PRAYING GOD'S WORD
FOR YOUR
BUSINESS

50 Prayers That Will
Transform Your Company

LOGAN BLOOM

PRAYERSHOP
PUBLISHING

Terre Haute, Indiana

PrayerShop Publishing is the publishing arm of the Church Prayer Leaders Network. The Church Prayer Leaders Network exists to equip and inspire local churches and their prayer leaders in their desire to disciple their people in prayer and to become a "house of prayer for all nations." Its online store, prayershop.org, has more than 150 prayer resources available for purchase or download.

ISBN (Print): 978-1-970176-04-9
ISBN (E-book): 978-1-970176-05-6

Scripture quotations are from
The ESV® Bible (The Holy Bible, English Standard Version®),
copyright © 2001 by Crossway, a publishing ministry of Good News Publishers.
Used by permission. All rights reserved.

1 2 3 4 5 | 2021 2022 2023 2024 2025

Table of Contents

Foreword

In my work with Christian business leaders all across America, I've seen the reality of Proverbs 16:3, which says, "Commit to the LORD whatever you do, and he will establish your plans" (NIV). We are skilled at committing our plans to him at the outset to get things "established," but we fail to see the need for his constant companionship and counsel to keep us aligned so that our plans are more than just successful at the beginning. We need his guidance to go the distance!

Have you ever wondered why a vigorous prayer life is one of the most common compromises we make in the Christian journey?

It is as though God gives us success here or positive movement there and we become convinced of the possibility that this world can provide us with what our heart longs for. These thoughts create a tension that presses against our prayer lives like a pallet of sandbags.

Speaking of sand, in Matthew 7 Jesus provides the juxtaposition of two men, one who builds his house on sand and the other the rock. Building a house on sand is faster, a far more rapid time to market. Building a house on the rock can feel laborious and it certainly slows down the completion of the project.

In the same way, prayer can seem like it is preventing us from getting down to business. But all the while, it is enabling us to build things that will stand the certain storms that this life will bring, both in business and in our personal lives.

Another tension that works against a vigorous prayer life is our gifting, skill, and talent. I've seen many leaders who have relied on their IQ, EQ, whit, and horse-sense so much that they begin to take the credit, believe their own press releases, and think that they have impressed God with how good they are. Don't misunderstand. These things can make a good leader, but they will fail to make a leader good. These things can fuel our pride and drive a life of independence from Christ. The result is an anemic prayer life.

As Christian business leaders, we must marvel at the reality that prayer is the conduit or channel to the very mind of Christ, the very throne of Grace. As you start this book, imagine Almighty God leaning in to hear what you have to say. Allow your heart to realize Psalm 116:2, which says, "Because he bends down to listen, I will pray as long as I have breath!" (NLT).

Some compare prayer in the spiritual life to breathing in physical life. While breathing is a natural, involuntary function, occurring with no thought, prayer *seems* to be the opposite. Seems is the keyword. I often find I think of prayer in its complexity more than its simplicity. The solution is bringing my problems before God with childlike faith and dependence, the very antithesis of a confident, competent leader in the 21st century.

Logan Bloom, like me, has been in the trenches with business leaders who were passionate for Jesus, but felt inadequate in prayer. As we've journeyed together with them, we've seen many develop a vigorous prayer life. And we've seen God's favor on their lives, families, and businesses. We've seen their hearts turn toward their employees, families, and communities in beautiful ways. We've heard the stories of unmerited favor, successful ventures, and fruitful projects as these business leaders invited Christ into the most intimate of details of their lives and companies. The impact of a vital prayer life in these business leaders' lives is undeniable.

Let me encourage you to embrace the discipline of using Logan's book. He designed it to be used as one of your first priorities each day. Arrange your schedule so there are no distractions. Jesus modeled this for us in his own life, as the Gospels note his early morning time, getting centered with the Father. In just a few short days, you will experience a heart connection with Jesus that produces fruit--like direction, fruitfulness, and peace in a storm. I believe you will quickly find that your prayer time becomes a day-long, running conversation with the Most-High God, just as Christ modeled. This will be the fulfillment of Jesus' prayer in John 17:23, that we would be one with him and the Father.

"I in them and you in me, that they may become perfectly one, so that the world may know that you sent me and loved them even as you loved me."

Consider how you can find real strength through prayers of dependence and transparency. Allow God to see what we all know is true. We are weak apart from him. The great news is that we are immeasurably strong with him! Even the Great Commission in Matthew 28:19-20 promises that as we fulfill God's purposes for our days, he will be with us for the entire journey.

My prayer for you is that this book enables you to (re)discover that the Lord is the most wonderful traveling companion for your life and business! As you meet regularly, you'll find him listening and guiding you to discover fruitful abundance through your daily, intimate conversations with the Almighty.

Larry Griffith, CEO
Corporate Chaplains of America

Introduction

"I didn't think that prayer would work," my friend admitted. He was a business owner who, like many of us, had always heard talk about prayer but struggled to pray. He felt that he couldn't afford to spend time in prayer.

Despite his best efforts, he fell more behind, grew more exhausted, and imagined Jesus as indifferent toward his work. Does that sound familiar?

His struggle is all too common among business leaders. We don't know how to pray for our business. We're too busy and too skeptical. When we finally do take a moment to pray, after exhausting every other option, we feel empty and discouraged.

That was when a small group of friends decided to meet together regularly to pray for each other's businesses. It was very challenging at first, but we were determined to give it a try for six months. We spent time at each meeting reading a short Scripture about Jesus' character, desire, and power toward us. It was not long before we realized that we had stumbled upon one of the deepest passions in the heart of Jesus. We began to uncover Jesus' desire to use our businesses in his redemptive plan.

The most unexpected things began to happen in the months that followed. "It is hard to explain," one business owner remarked, "but prayer became the most profitable use of my time. Prayer set every hour of my workweek into order, released my anxiety, and changed my productivity. I made better decisions when I prayed. It has gotten to the point where it would be irresponsible not to pray for my business! I can't believe I didn't do this sooner."

The most remarkable result was how each member of the group grew more confident in their relationship with Jesus. Their prayers were answered not just with provision, but with an invitation to be part of something greater than we had imagined. As word began to spread, our groups began to multiply. We started to dream about the potential impact of a community of business leaders who shared this vision and experience. It seemed like such a radical idea at first, but we soon realized that such a movement has always been the intention of Jesus for business.

For some, this may sound familiar, but I want to welcome those for whom this is a new idea. Maybe God has already placed a hunger in your heart to see your city impacted by a growing community of praying business leaders. Chances are you are not the only one. Prayer has preceded every move of God in history. Perhaps in the reading of this book, you could be the spark for your church or your city. May this book be fuel for your fire.

Why Should I Pray for My Business?

How precious to me are your thoughts, O God! How vast is the sum of them! If I would count them, they are more than the sand. (Psalm 139:17–18)

Have you ever wondered what Jesus may think about your work? It may not seem like a big question at first, but this is one of the most important questions that you will ever ask. Yes, Jesus does think about your work, but do you know what he thinks? Prayer is the process by which your thoughts come into alignment with his thoughts. Many people spend their entire lives disconnected from the thoughts of Jesus, and in doing so relegate their potential to their limited understanding and strength. Meanwhile, we miss out on the perfect wisdom and limitless strength of Jesus.

Now to him who is able to do far more abundantly than all that we ask or think . . . (Ephesians 3:20)

We serve a heavenly Father whose power exceeds our expectations in every way. You are incapable of overestimating his ability to act for you and through you with the full resources of heaven. Imagine that! No situation is too big or too small for him. Notice that Paul is not only referring to our heavenly Father in this verse, but he also refers to us. We have a responsibility to ask and imagine, to pray with faith. We can't do his part for him, and he won't do our part for us. The prayer of faith is the first step to experience the power of God in your work.

Ask, and it will be given to you; seek, and you will find; knock, and it will be opened to you. For everyone who asks receives, and the one who seeks finds, and to the one who knocks it will be opened. Or which one of you, if his son asks him for bread, will give him a stone? Or if he asks for a fish, will give him a serpent? If you then, who are evil, know how to give good gifts to your children, how much more will your Father who is in heaven give good things to those who ask him! (Matthew 7:7–11)

Jesus told his disciples to pray without reservation, and he demonstrated the importance of prayer in his daily life. Think of that: even Jesus needed to pray. Earlier in this same message (Matthew 6:8), Jesus explained how our heavenly Father knows what we need before we ask him, but he still tells us to ask. Thankfully, we serve a good heavenly Father. Even our best efforts could never match his goodness toward us. We can pray with confidence that God enjoys our prayers and takes delight in providing for us.

You desire and do not have, so you murder. You covet and cannot obtain, so you fight and quarrel. You do not have, because you do not ask. You ask and do not receive, because you ask wrongly, to spend it on your passions. (James 4:2–3)

There is some provision that we do not receive unless we ask for it in prayer. There may be areas of your work where you have never felt the need to pray for provision. If that is the case, then your thoughts have likely been far too small when compared to the thoughts of Jesus. The thoughts of Jesus always include an element of risk that drives us to depend on him. When we assume the risk and come into alignment with his thoughts, then our prayers release provision that simply awaited our request.

Do not be anxious about anything, but in everything by prayer and supplication with thanksgiving let your requests be made known to God. (Philippians 4:6)

If you have ever wondered what circumstance qualifies for prayer, here is the answer: everything. Paul did not say "once you've tried everything else," or "when it gets really bad"; he said, "in everything." Pray whenever you want God to be involved. You may be thinking, *I always want God to be involved.* Exactly! Just as you would not withhold your greatest advantage from your business, prayer should be your first resort.

We pray when there's nothing else we can do, but God wants us to pray before we do anything at all. (Oswald Chambers)

Business leaders everywhere are exhausting themselves to gain a competitive advantage in a world of limited resources. Meanwhile, Scripture speaks of a heavenly economy of unlimited resource that transcends natural economic laws. To Jesus money is literally no object, and his economy has a purpose far beyond any worldly standard of living. Its resources are material, but its results are eternal. Jesus is in the business of restoring people, and it's a family business! Technicians and engineers, entrepreneurs and artists, gig workers and brokers, janitors and CEOs—we are all involved in his redemptive work.

Prayer is the primary means by which we grow in relationship with Jesus and in partnership with his work. Growing closer to Jesus in prayer means becoming a better leader, a better parent and spouse, and a better friend. In prayer we put off our old selves and are remade in his likeness. In prayer we release our fears and receive his delight. In prayer we quiet the noise to hear his wisdom. In prayer we overcome worldly limitations and engage his infinite economy. It is our direct, unlimited access to our greatest resource at a moment's notice. As we grow in relationship with Jesus and partnership with his work, we become a vessel through which he can demonstrate his power.

What Does Prayer Look Like?

This is the best part: the power of our prayers is not determined by how they sound or look. The power of our prayers is fixed securely in Jesus, transcendent of time, space, and resource. The simplicity of prayer is one of the reasons why it is often overlooked, but its simplicity means that it can be adjusted to fit any situation. Jesus can accomplish more in five seconds of prayer than we could accomplish in five lifetimes. It can happen in the car on the way to the job site, in the moments before your next meeting, or during your next phone call. It can happen in one minute, one hour, or several hours. Your prayers do not have to be a certain length or perfectly worded. Even our weakest prayers are of great value to Jesus.

Prayer is an ongoing dialog that is not often one-sided. You can make a habit of praying in your own words throughout your daily life, leaving them open-ended as a continual dialog. Be sure to take pauses to listen—Jesus is always ready to speak to those who have ears to hear. Find a rhythm that works for you and follow the prompting of the Holy Spirit.

Over time, you will experience answers to prayer that build your faith. King David was a lowly shepherd boy in his youth, but God helped him fend off lions and bears while defending his sheep. David grew stronger in faith with each victory until the day that he faced Goliath. Answered prayers build our faith in the same way. You will build a similar history with Jesus in prayer as you learn to recognize his voice and understand his leadership.

Do not let the simplicity of prayer trick you into thinking that prayer is easy. Prayer can be a trying experience even for the mature believer. You might be tempted to think that your prayers are ineffective if you don't feel anything when you pray. We can be confident that Jesus is moved by our prayers even when we don't feel moved by them. Everyone faces difficulty getting started, so consider these suggestions as you begin your journey.

Tips for Getting Started

There is really only one way to grow in prayer: by praying! Getting started can be an uphill battle, especially for the busy-minded among us. Here are a few practical steps that you can take to jumpstart your prayer time. These are not rigid rules, but they may give you an advantage when distraction inevitably comes knocking. Understand, the devil will do everything in his power to disrupt your prayer time. Let that be an encouragement to you to prioritize prayer all the more.

Schedule Time for Prayer

There are many demands on your time. Experience has proven that those who set a consistent time to pray tend to experience better results than those who "just wing it." Scheduling a protected time for prayer demonstrates its priority and gives you a chance to really focus. Of course, you will not keep your schedule 100% of the time, but you will keep it more often than not. You don't have to schedule a long length of time. It could be ten minutes at the start of your day, or an hour per week, but pick something doable and start from there. You can easily tweak your schedule at times to keep it working with other things in your life.

Make a Prayer List

Start developing a simple prayer list for your business. *Praying God's Word for Your Business* is both a book of prayer starters *and* a journal. There is space here to write down your requests. This tool can help you focus during your prayer times, especially when your mind is blank and needs a jump start. You don't have to limit your prayers to items on the list but use it simply as a guide. Feel free to depart from your list if you feel inspired to pray differently and return to it anytime. You're far more likely to overcome dry spells with a prayer list.

Each prayer in this resource has a section at the end of the prayer for you to write down your thoughts in three key areas:

- **Reflect:** In your own words, thank God for where you have seen his provision and express your commitment to honor him in everything.

- **Request:** In your own words, make your needs known to God. He knows our needs but still invites us to ask.

- **Rely:** In your own words, express your commitment to God's leadership and his glory with the outcome.

At the top of your list, each day, ask Jesus to reveal his purpose for your business. This is often a lifelong prayer request. My personal list contains the following permanent item: *Align me with Your desire and empower me to accomplish it today.* Allocate a portion of your time to praying over your purpose statement for your business. This is an excellent opportunity to listen for God's whispers as he guides your thoughts. Then, over time, keep that purpose statement at the top of your list and continue to develop it.

Don't be afraid to be specific in your list. Your prayers are like the stones in David's sling, targeting the giants facing your business. God honors specific prayers with specific answers. Include the quarterly, monthly, or weekly needs of your business and everything that keeps you up at night. Then update your list as time passes. Mark answered prayers and add new ones. Pretty soon your prayer list will be a journal of answered prayer. Here are three simple common themes that can help categorize your list.

1. **Prayer for the gifts of the Holy Spirit:** Pray for a greater release of the gifts of the Holy Spirit, including God's power, favor, provision, and protection. You can pray for a greater measure of the gifts of the Holy Spirit to be manifest in your business and community.

2. **Prayer for the fruit of the Holy Spirit:** Pray for a greater release of the fruit of the Holy Spirit in Galatians 5:22–23 and for God's character to be formed in your business and community.

3. **Prayer for the wisdom of the Holy Spirit:** Pray for a greater release of the wisdom of the Holy Spirit and an increase of understanding and insight into God's plans, will, and Word for your business and community.

Remember your prayers; ask the Lord for opportunities to act on them. You may be surprised by the number of prayers that Jesus uses you to answer. Learn to recognize the opportunities that arise as a result of your prayers. As you get into the habit of prayer, you will begin to recognize his leadership and activity in increasing ways.

To some, scheduling a time and making a list may feel legalistic. It can be, but it does not have to be. Setting regular times for prayer and using a prayer list are simply a reflection of our desire to make prayer a priority.

Study Jesus' Heart for Your Business

If I could encourage you with one key takeaway, if you could learn one thing, if there is one thing that keeps us going and makes our prayers effective, it is the constant pursuit to understand the heart of Jesus. Cultivating a right view of Jesus is the primary ingredient of effective prayer.

As you read the Scriptures included in this book, study what they reveal about Jesus. That is why they are there. Too many believers avoid prayer simply because of a wrong view of Jesus. You may think that Jesus is detached and indifferent toward your work or standing ready to condemn you. These could not be further from the truth. *Impersonal* and *indifferent* are not attributes of Jesus toward you or your work. We do not have to twist his arm into answering our prayers. Our prayer lives become very different with the assurance that he enjoys us as we grow. A right view of Jesus causes us to want to pray.

Pray with Others

Prayer is not antisocial—in fact, the opposite is true. Prayer is always strengthened by community, and vice versa. Find two or three other business leaders to pray with you or gather a few colleagues at the office. You will keep your prayer time more often when it is shared with others. This is not to say that you should only pray in groups. More often than not the group context is neglected as we all secretly struggle to pray. Jesus designed us for community, and the same is true of prayer. Your prayer life and your relationships will be stronger when you pray with others.

Do Not Be Discouraged

For the eyes of the Lord run to and fro throughout the whole earth, to give strong support to those whose heart is blameless toward him. (2 Chronicles 16:9)

What sort of qualifications do you think Jesus considers when including someone in his work? We know the standards that *we* generally seek: a particular education, job experience, or other accomplishments. We definitely know the standards held by the IRS and the banks. The eyes of the Lord search the earth for people of a certain heart posture. The posture of your heart speaks of your attitude toward Jesus and toward others. When Jesus finds a heart that is truly surrendered to him and vibrant in love, then he has found a vessel for his work.

As you begin this journey, understand that working with Jesus is not always what you expect. Our world is concerned primarily with quick success and material possessions. The work of Jesus is beyond all of that in the unseen thoughts of the heart. Jesus is in the business of restoring people inside *and* out, but your heart is his first priority. When his desires become your desires, your heart becomes free. Jesus promises to demonstrate his power over worldly wealth through people over which worldly wealth has no power.

I emphasize this point in hopes that your heart may find stability when you face difficult circumstances. Jesus does not promise to withhold difficult circumstances from our lives, but he does promise to use them for his redemptive work. You can imagine the threat that a prayerful business leader poses to the kingdom of darkness. There are few things the devil fears more than an unshakable business leader to whom Jesus can direct resources for the restoration of the world. Rest assured that you will face giants—but take heart, Jesus has already won!

I have said these things to you, that in me you may have peace. In the world you will have tribulation. But take heart; I have overcome the world. (John 16:33)

Take Inventory

A good exercise to complete before you begin praying through this guide, is to "take inventory" of the past and your dreams for the future of your business. I highly recommend spending some time both contemplating and writing down your answers to the following questions:

Prior to now, how much have you recognized God at work in your business?

_____

_____

_____

_____

_____

_____

_____

_____

Have you recognized answered prayer in your work before now? If so, list some examples.

_____

_____

_____

_____

_____

_____

_____

_____

What do you imagine that God thinks about your business?

_____

_____

_____

_____

_____

_____

_____

_____

_____

_____

In your own words, what would you say is God's purpose for your business?

_____

_____

_____

_____

_____

_____

_____

_____

_____

_____

_____

If you could ask God for insight regarding one particular thing, what would it be?

_____

_____

_____

_____

_____

_____

Now take a moment to look ahead to your business goals over the next 6 months.

Use the following space to create a list of the major obstacles that need to be overcome and the opportunities that need to be leveraged to achieve those goals. What are the giants immediately in front of you that keep you up at night? Be specific! Your prayers for this list will be like David's stones in his sling. Consider inviting a few other business leaders to embark on this journey with you. You can all share periodic updates to pray for needs and celebrate progress. We will follow up on these answers on page 122.

_____

_____

_____

_____

_____

_____

_____

_____

_____

1

● **Provision**
● **Direction**

Psalm 67:1-2, 6

May God be gracious to us and bless us and make his face to shine upon us, that your way may be known on earth, your saving power among all nations. . . . The earth has yielded its increase; God, our God, shall bless us.

Reflect: _____

_____

_____

_____

_____

_____

_____

_____

Request: _____

_____

_____

_____

_____

_____

Heavenly Father,

Thank you for your goodness.
I ask for your blessing on my business today.

Be gracious in your leadership toward me,
my co-workers, and my employees.

Bless our work, bless our decisions, and bless our people.

Let your face shine upon us so that others
would look at our business and glorify you.

Use my business to draw people to yourself
as an example of your saving power.

May we represent you well today in everything we do.

I commit myself to your purpose for my work
and invite you to be part of this business.

Provide for our needs according to Your strength
and lead us according to Your will.

In the mighty name of Jesus, Amen.

———————

Rely:

PRAYER

2

Provision
Direction

Psalm 90:16-17

Let Your work be shown to Your servants,
and Your glorious power to their children.
Let the favor of the Lord our God be upon us,
and establish the work of our hands upon us;
yes, establish the work of our hands!

Reflect:

Request:

Heavenly Father,

Thank you for your provision this week.

Show me where you are at work in my business.
May my business demonstrate your glorious power
to my employees, customers and community.

Place your favor on every aspect of our work.
Give us the opportunity to represent you well in all that we do.

Establish the work of our hands and give us greater productivity
and efficiency than we could ever achieve on our own.

Bless me to give you the glory with my business.
I invite you into my work.

Provide for our needs according to Your strength
and lead us according to your will.

In the mighty name of Jesus, Amen.

———————●———————

Rely:_____

_____

_____

_____

_____

_____

_____

_____

PRAYER

3

- **Wisdom**
- **Strength**

Colossians 1:9-11

And so, from the day we heard, we have not ceased to pray for you, asking that you may be filled with the knowledge of his will in all spiritual wisdom and understanding, so as to walk in a manner worthy of the Lord, fully pleasing to him: bearing fruit in every good work and increasing in the knowledge of God; being strengthened with all power, according to his glorious might, for all endurance and patience with joy.

Reflect: _____

_____

_____

_____

_____

_____

Request: _____

_____

_____

_____

_____

Heavenly Father,

Thank you for your provision this week.

Reveal your will for this business to me.

Let me see my work and my people as you see them.

Fill me with your wisdom and understanding,
and help me to trust your leadership above my own strength.

Empower me and my business to bear good fruit
in every circumstance, especially in our relationships.

Strengthen me, my business and my people
according to your power, not our own.

May we be faithful stewards and ambassadors
with the endurance, patience and joy that comes from you.

I invite you to be part of this business.

Provide for our needs according to your strength
and lead us according to your will.

In the mighty name of Jesus, Amen.

Rely:

PRAYER

4

● Provision

Isaiah 45:2-3, 5-6

I [the Lord] will go before you
and level the exalted places,
I will break in pieces the doors of bronze
 and cut through the bars of iron,
I will give you the treasures of darkness
and the hoards in secret places,
that you may know that it is I, the Lord,
the God of Israel, who call you by your
name. . . .
I am the Lord, and there is no other,
besides me there is no God;
I equip you . . . that people may know, from
the rising of the sun
and from the west, that . . . I am the Lord,
and there is no other.

Reflect: _____

_____

_____

_____

Request: _____

_____

_____

_____

Heavenly Father,

Thank you for your provision.

Give me your favor in my business this week.

Prepare my path ahead of me and help me
overcome areas of strife in my work.

Show me your greater wisdom for my business.

Equip my people and me to be prepared for our work both
physically, mentally and spiritually.

Give us the strength to serve you well.

Above all, may you receive the glory.
I pray that your divine purpose would prevail and that others would
look at my business and see you.

Be strong in us and through us as we represent you to the world.
I invite you to be part of this business.

Provide for our needs according to your strength
and lead us according to your will.

In the mighty name of Jesus, Amen.

———————●———————

Rely: _____

_____

_____

_____

_____

PRAYER

5

▪ Hope

1 Timothy 6:17

As for the rich in this present age, charge them not to be haughty, nor to set their hopes on the uncertainty of riches, but on God, who richly provides us with everything to enjoy.

Reflect: _____

_____

_____

_____

_____

_____

_____

Request: _____

_____

_____

_____

_____

_____

_____

Heavenly Father,

Thank you for your goodness and kindness this week.
Your leadership is perfect and your will is steadfast.

Forgive me for the times that I set my hope
in material positions or my account balance.

You are my provider and I place my trust in you.
Whether I have much or little,
I know that you are always with me.

Thank you for providing for my family
and for the opportunities of this week.
You are good and your promises are true.

Help me not to give the devil a foothold of false trust.
I release those footholds of anxiety and stress
that stem from misplaced trust.

May this be a business that trusts in you
and reflects your goodness in all we do.

In the mighty name of Jesus, Amen.

Rely: _____

_____

_____

_____

_____

_____

PRAYER

6

▪ Wisdom

Ephesians 1:17-19

[I pray] that the God of our Lord Jesus Christ, the Father of glory, may give you the Spirit of wisdom and of revelation in the knowledge of him, having the eyes of your hearts enlightened, that you may know what is the hope to which he has called you, what are the riches of his glorious inheritance in the saints, and what is the immeasurable greatness of his power toward us who believe, according to the working of his great might.

Reflect: _____

_____

_____

_____

_____

_____

Request: _____

_____

_____

_____

_____

Heavenly Father,

Thank you for your goodness to me.

You deserve all of the glory
for the growth of my business.

Fill me with your Spirit today
and give me your wisdom for my work.

Help me not to lean only on my own understanding
but to trust your ways. I want to see your perspective
and be led by your Spirit in every decision.

Give me and my employees
the spirit of revelation in the knowledge of you.
Help us to grow closer to you and to see your work in us.

Empower us to do business not only for you but with you.

Use us to draw others to you and
be glorified by our work this week.

In the mighty name of Jesus, Amen.

———————●———————

Rely:_____

_____

_____

_____

_____

_____

PRAYER

7

Ephesians 1:17-19

- **Direction**
- **Hope**

*I pray that the God of our Lord Jesus Christ, the Father of glory, may give you the Spirit of wisdom and of revelation in the knowledge of him, **having the eyes of your hearts enlightened, that you may know what is the hope to which he has called you, what are the riches of his glorious inheritance in the saints,** and what is the immeasurable greatness of his power toward us who believe, according to the working of his great might.*

Reflect: _____

_____

_____

_____

_____

Request: _____

_____

_____

_____

_____

_____

Heavenly Father,

Thank you for your provision this week.

Open my eyes to see where you are at work.
Help me to recognize your gentle leading and provision.

I don't want to miss any opportunity that you send my way. Show me the hope of your calling for me and my business.

Make my company a conduit for hope in people's lives.

Help me to understand how my business can be
part of your greater purpose in my sphere of influence.

Remove anything that would distract me from your calling and
provide for our needs according
to the riches of your glorious inheritance.

I commit my business to you anew today.
Be glorified in my work this week.

In the mighty name of Jesus, Amen.

Rely: _____

_____

_____

_____

_____

_____

PRAYER

8

● Provision

Ephesians 1:17–19

I pray that the God of our Lord Jesus Christ, the Father of glory, may give you the Spirit of wisdom and of revelation in the knowledge of him, having the eyes of your hearts enlightened, that you may know what is the hope to which he has called you, what are the riches of his glorious inheritance in the saints, **and what is the immeasurable greatness of his power toward us who believe, according to the working of his great might.**

Reflect: _____

_____

_____

_____

_____

_____

Request: _____

_____

_____

_____

_____

Heavenly Father,

Thank you for hearing my prayers.

Thank you for all the ways that you have
watched over me and provided for me.

I commit myself to your greater purpose for my business
and I pray that your will would prosper here.

Use my business to demonstrate your power
to my employees and customers.

Let me be a testimony to others of your
faithfulness and provision.

I confess that my strength is not strong enough.
May this business be characterized by your strength, not mine.

Provide for us according to your infinite resource
and your perfect will.

I pray that when others see this business
that they would see you.
Be glorified in us and through us this week.

In the mighty name of Jesus, Amen.

Rely:_____

_____

_____

_____

_____

_____

PRAYER

9

- **Hope**
- **Protection**

Isaiah 54:17

No weapon that is fashioned against you shall succeed,

and you shall refute every tongue that rises against you in judgment.

This is the heritage of the servants of the LORD

and their vindication from me, declares the LORD.

Reflect: _____

_____

_____

_____

_____

_____

_____

Request: _____

_____

_____

_____

_____

Heavenly Father,

Thank you for your protection,
for your victory in Jesus, and the gift of your Holy Spirit.

This is ultimately your business and your work.

Cause every weapon of the enemy
formed against this business to fail.

Deliver us from every attack and accusation
that the devil uses to detract from your purpose.

I set my hope in you alone.
Strengthen my heart not to give a foothold
to fear when my enemy opposes my work.

Give me the confidence to stand firm in the storms
as a source of stability to my business.

Be glorified in our victories and show the world
your strength in our weakness.

Thank you for this promise
that we receive today as your people.

In the mighty name of Jesus, Amen.

———————

Rely:_____

_____

_____

_____

_____

_____

PRAYER
10

● **Strength**

Ephesians 3:16-19

That according to the riches of his glory
he may grant you to be strengthened with
power through his Spirit in your inner being,
so that Christ may dwell in your hearts
through faith—that you, being rooted and
grounded in love, may have strength to
comprehend with all the saints what is the
breadth and length and height and depth,
and to know the love of Christ that surpasses
knowledge, that you may be filled with all the
fullness of God.

Reflect: _____

_____

_____

_____

_____

Request: _____

_____

_____

_____

_____

Heavenly Father,

Thank you for your kindness towards me this week.

I ask that your strength would be
displayed in my business this week.
Make us an example of your strength, not ours.

Strengthen me, my family, my employees, and my customers.
Give us the energy and focus to do your work with excellence.

Cause our circumstances to work in our favor
and every attack of the enemy to fail.

Keep us in good health, both physically and mentally.

Provide for us according to riches of your glory
and lead us with your Spirit.

I pray that every person in this business
would be aligned with your greater purpose:
that Christ may dwell in our hearts through faith.

Fill us with your Spirit, strengthen us with your power,
and use us to draw people to you this week.

In the mighty name of Jesus, Amen.

Rely:

PRAYER

11

Strength

Ephesians 3:16-19

*That according to the riches of his glory he may grant you to be strengthened with power through his Spirit in your inner being, so that Christ may dwell in your hearts through faith—**that you, being rooted and grounded in love, may have strength to comprehend with all the saints what is the breadth and length and height and depth, and to know the love of Christ that surpasses knowledge, that you may be filled with all the fullness of God.***

Reflect: _____

_____

_____

_____

_____

Request: _____

_____

_____

_____

_____

_____

Heavenly Father,

Thank you for your unending love.

Help me to understand your love better
and display it to those around me.

I want to see my work as you see it.
Show me the breadth and length
and height and depth of your love toward us.

Make my business rooted and grounded in your love.
Let your love pass beyond something we know about
to something that we experience.

I don't want to settle for less than your fullness for my business.
Remove every hindrance to your purpose so that
we can experience everything you have for us.

Help me to lead with love
and put your love on display
in my business this week.

In the mighty name of Jesus, Amen.

———————●———————

Rely:_____

_____

_____

_____

_____

_____

12

- **Provision**
- **Protection**

Matthew 10:29-32

Are not two sparrows sold for a penny? And not one of them will fall to the ground apart from your Father. But even the hairs of your head are all numbered. Fear not, therefore; you are of more value than many sparrows. So everyone who acknowledges me before men, I also will acknowledge before my Father who is in heaven.

Reflect: _____

_____

_____

_____

_____

_____

Request: _____

_____

_____

_____

_____

Heavenly Father,

Thank you for watching over me.

Show me how to value each of my employees
and customers the way that you value them.

Cause my business to be a source of affirmation
for the care that you have for them.

Help me to have confidence in your watchfulness.
You are my ultimate security.

Replace my anxiety with renewed faith.

Make your provision so clear that others
will recognize it and see your goodness.

Make my business one that acknowledges you
not in words only, but in our conduct.

I commit to give you the glory as I join my prayers to yours.

Release the fullness of your provision
and be glorified in us this week.

In the mighty name of Jesus, Amen.

———————◼———————

Rely:_____

_____

_____

_____

_____

_____

13

- **Provision**
- **Strength**

1 Chronicles 29:11–12

Yours, O LORD, is the greatness and the power and the glory and the victory and the majesty, for all that is in the heavens and in the earth is yours. Yours is the kingdom, O LORD, and you are exalted as head above all. Both riches and honor come from you, and you rule over all. In your hand are power and might, and in your hand it is to make great and to give strength to all.

Reflect: _____

_____

_____

_____

_____

Request: _____

_____

_____

_____

_____

Heavenly Father,

Thank you for your sovereignty over my business.
Today, I acknowledge that my business is in your hands.

Every opportunity that I have to bless someone's life with my
business comes from your hand and for your glory.

Be exalted as head above all in my business.

Make my business a testimony of your
greatness, power, and glory.

Provide for each of our needs
according to your power and might.

Show me how to lead with your wisdom and strength
for the kind of success that only comes from you.

Work through us in such a way that others
would see miracles that only you could do.

Use us to bless the lives of everyone we interact with
and to show your goodness to the world.

We want to make your name great this week.

In the mighty name of Jesus, Amen.

Rely:_____

_____

_____

_____

_____

PRAYER

14

● **Unity**

Romans 15:5-6

May the God of endurance and encouragement grant you to live in such harmony with one another, in accord with Christ Jesus, that together you may with one voice glorify the God and Father of our Lord Jesus Christ.

Reflect: _____

_____

_____

_____

_____

_____

Request: _____

_____

_____

_____

_____

_____

Heavenly Father,

Thank you for your never-ending faithfulness.

I give you praise today because I know that your plans
are for my good and encouragement.

I trust in your plans, even in uncertainty and turmoil.

Give me faith and endurance to persevere in my work.

Encourage me and my business this week.
I want to represent you well, even when it is difficult.

Help me find ways to encourage those around me,
just as you encourage me.

Bring harmony to my business and our relationships
with our employees, vendors, and customers.
Remove divisiveness and confusion and
give us clarity in our work.

Cast far from us anything that hinders our ability
as a business to glorify you.

May the culture of our business
point everyone straight to you.

In the mighty name of Jesus, Amen.

———————●———————

Rely:_____

_____

_____

_____

_____

PRAYER

15

- **Wisdom**
- **Hope**

Proverbs 3:13-16

Blessed is the one who finds wisdom,
and the one who gets understanding,
for the gain from her is better than gain from
silver and her profit better than gold.
She is more precious than jewels,
and nothing you desire can compare with her.
Long life is in her right hand;
in her left hand are riches and honor.

Reflect: _____

_____

_____

_____

_____

_____

Request: _____

_____

_____

_____

_____

Heavenly Father,

Thank you for sustaining me this week.

Give me your wisdom that supersedes my thinking.

Show me the wisdom that produces
the greatest result in every circumstance.

I want my business to be known for
a profit greater than silver or gold.

Make me teachable in every situation
so that I may grow into the transformative leader
that you have called me to be.

Show me how to be humble in success, faithful in the storms,
and always allowing your will to prosper.

Give me your perspective and help me to
make clear and right decisions.
I put my hope and trust in you.

Your leadership is perfect, and your wisdom is eternal.

Fill my business with your Spirit as our greatest provision.

Be glorified through our resources, our reputation,
and your wisdom in our decisions this week.

In the mighty name of Jesus, Amen.

———————●———————

Rely:_____

_____

_____

PRAYER

16

- **Provision**
- **Direction**

Isaiah 55:8-10

For my thoughts are not your thoughts,
neither are your ways my ways, declares
the Lord.
For as the heavens are higher than the
earth,
so are my ways higher than your ways
and my thoughts than your thoughts.
[I cause] the rain and the snow come down
from heaven . . . [and] water the earth,
making it bring forth and sprout,
giving seed to the sower and bread to the
eater.

Reflect: _____

_____

_____

_____

_____

Request: _____

_____

_____

_____

Heavenly Father,

Thank you for your guidance this week.

I confess that your ways are higher than my ways,
and your leadership is better than mine.

Help my leadership to become more like yours,
according to your eternal values.

Give me your perspective for my work and make me sensitive to
the promptings of your Holy Spirit.

I want my business to display your character in all that we do.

Let us be an example of leadership that is greater
than ours to our employees, vendors, and customers.

The ultimate provision for my business comes from you.
Cause your rain to fall on us and provide for our business.
In your wisdom, make us fruitful.

Show me clearly how to steward your provision
for the best possible result.

Guide me on how to invest, how to be generous,
and how to provide for my family and my employees.

Demonstrate the greatness of your ways
so that we may glorify you brightly this week.

In the mighty name of Jesus, Amen.

Rely:_____

_____

_____

17

- **Wisdom**
- **Direction**

Proverbs 16:3, 9

Commit your work to the Lord, and your plans will be established. . . . The heart of man plans his way, but the Lord establishes his steps.

Reflect: _____

_____

_____

_____

Request: _____

_____

_____

_____

_____

Rely: _____

_____

_____

_____

Heavenly Father,

Thank you for your goodness this week.

I desire to commit my work to you.
Show me how to take the next step.

I invite you to be involved in each plan,
each decision, and each job.

Help me to commit each moment to you.

More than a slogan, I want this to be
the culture of my business.

I can spend every minute of today making plans,
but this is the moment when you establish my steps.
Lead me in the way I should go.

I trust you for the connections and resources that we need.

Establish us in your will.
Help me not to assume responsibility
for what you have done,
but to always acknowledge you.

This is ultimately your business,
so make your name great through us.

I commit the plans for this week to you.

Have your way, and receive the greatest glory this week.

In the mighty name of Jesus, Amen.

PRAYER

18

- **Peace**
- **Direction**

Proverbs 3:5-10

Trust in the Lord with all your heart,
and do not lean on your own understanding.
In all your ways acknowledge him,
and he will make straight your paths.
Be not wise in your own eyes;
fear the Lord, and turn away from evil.
It will be healing to your flesh
and refreshment to your bones.
Honor the Lord with your wealth
and with the firstfruits of all your produce;
then your barns will be filled with plenty,
and your vats will be bursting with wine.

Reflect: _____

_____

_____

_____

_____

Request: _____

_____

_____

_____

_____

Heavenly Father,

Thank you for hearing my prayers.

I admit there are times when
it is difficult to trust you in my business.

Help me not to run so quickly to my own understanding
or rely on my own strength in moments of pressure.

I need your peace in the midst of the storms.

Give me the grace to trust you more with my business.
Help me to put more trust in you than in my bank statement.

I place the challenges facing my business at your feet
and ask for your help and guidance.

Speak to me in the quiet moments of the day.

Lead me in how I should work and make my path straight.

Make my business a testimony of your wisdom and power
so that people would see our success and glorify you.

I put my trust in you this week.

In the mighty name of Jesus, Amen.

———————●———————

Rely:_____

_____

_____

_____

_____

PRAYER

19

● Wisdom

Proverbs 3:5-10

Trust in the Lord with all your heart,
and do not lean on your own understanding.
In all your ways acknowledge him,
and he will make straight your paths.
Be not wise in your own eyes;
fear the Lord, and turn away from evil.
It will be healing to your flesh
and refreshment to your bones.
Honor the Lord with your wealth
and with the firstfruits of all your produce;
then your barns will be filled with plenty,
and your vats will be bursting with wine.

Reflect: _____

_____

_____

_____

_____

Request: _____

_____

_____

_____

_____

Heavenly Father,

Thank you for your provision this week.

Help me not to be wise in my own eyes.
Show me areas of my business where
I have trusted in my wisdom above yours.

I want to be wise in your sight and
humble in your presence.

Guard me against being reactionary in my work
and help me to be quick to trust you.

Show me the areas where the devil
has sought a foothold in my business.

I want to honor you with all of my work.
Help me and my people to act rightly and turn away
from evil in every circumstance.

We want to be the salt and light of the world.
Refresh us and give us strength as we work to honor you.

Let your wisdom be like healing power to us
and all with whom we work this week.

In the mighty name of Jesus, Amen.

Rely:

● **Provision**
● **Direction**

Proverbs 3:5-10

Trust in the Lord with all your heart,
and do not lean on your own understanding.
In all your ways acknowledge him,
and he will make straight your paths.
Be not wise in your own eyes;
fear the Lord, and turn away from evil.
It will be healing to your flesh
and refreshment to your bones.
Honor the Lord with your wealth
and with the firstfruits of all your produce;
then your barns will be filled with plenty,
and your vats will be bursting with wine.

Reflect: _____

_____

_____

_____

_____

Request: _____

_____

_____

_____

_____

Heavenly Father,

Thank you for dealing generously with me.

Your goodness and provision extend far beyond what I deserve.

You even know my needs before I ask, yet you delight in my asking.

Show me how to honor you with the firstfruits of my business.

I want the fullness of what you have for me,
so I commit to obey your word to give in faith.

Lead me in how to be generous as you have been generous to me.

Speak to me about your purpose for the resources and the
relationships that you have so graciously given me.

I bring the needs of this week to you and ask for your help.

As I honor you with my business,
make us an example of your generosity and provision.

Provide for our needs and the needs of our families.

Use my business to advance your kingdom
and bless those around us.

Put your goodness on display as we honor you with our giving.

In the mighty name of Jesus, Amen.

———————

Rely:_____

_____

_____

_____

PRAYER

21

- **Peace**
- **Direction**

Haggai 2:7-9

And I will shake all nations, so that the treasures of all nations shall come in, and I will fill this house with glory, says the LORD of hosts. The silver is mine, and the gold is mine, declares the LORD of hosts. The latter glory of this house shall be greater than the former, says the LORD of hosts. And in this place I will give peace, declares the LORD of hosts.

Reflect: _____

_____

_____

_____

_____

Request: _____

_____

_____

_____

_____

Heavenly Father,

Thank you for your goodness.
Thank you for your perfect leadership.

I thank you for your desire to use businesses
like mine for the redemption of the world.

Help me to see my part in your redemptive plan.

May my business bring glory to your house
and be a blessing to your people.

Help me to trust you better and have confidence in your plan.

All of the world's resources are yours, including my business.

I lay my business at your feet and acknowledge your
ultimate ownership. Use it for your glory above everything else.

Give your peace to my business, to every relationship,
to every transaction, to every customer, and to me.

Mark my business with the peace that comes from you.

Make your plan increasingly clear to me and all with whom I work.

Provide for us as only you can, and use me
to accomplish your purpose this week.

In the mighty name of Jesus, Amen.

———————————●———————————

Rely: _____

_____

_____

PRAYER

22

- **Provision**
- **Direction**

2 Corinthians 9:10-12

He who supplies seed to the sower and bread for food will supply and multiply your seed for sowing and increase the harvest of your righteousness. You will be enriched in every way to be generous in every way, which through us will produce thanksgiving to God. For the ministry of this service is not only supplying the needs of the saints but is also overflowing in many thanksgivings to God.

Reflect: _____

_____

_____

_____

_____

Request: _____

_____

_____

_____

_____

Heavenly Father,

Thank you for your generosity towards me.
Every good thing of mine has come from you.

Thank you for providing for our needs and our giving.

I invite you to distinguish what you have provided
as bread for our needs and seed to give to your kingdom.

Guide me in where to give of the seed that you have given me.

Help me to recognize giving as part of your
greater purpose for the resources entrusted to me.

Use my resources for your kingdom.
I want to see provision through your eyes.

May my obedience to your prompting produce
a harvest of righteousness with eternal impact.

Let me be part of a wave of thanksgiving
that would begin today with generosity.

Lead me to give where you will be glorified.

In the mighty name of Jesus, Amen.

———■———

Rely:_____

_____

_____

_____

_____

_____

PRAYER

23

Matthew 6:31-33

- **Provision**
- **Peace**

Therefore do not be anxious, saying, "What shall we eat?" or "What shall we drink?" or "What shall we wear?" For the Gentiles seek after all these things, and your heavenly Father knows that you need them all. But seek first the kingdom of God and his righteousness, and all these things will be added to you.

Reflect: _____

_____

_____

_____

_____

_____

_____

Request: _____

_____

_____

_____

_____

_____

_____

Heavenly Father,

Thank you for always providing for me.

I acknowledge my dependence on you
and remember the ways that you have
proven yourself to be faithful.

Help me to trust you in times of uncertainty in my business.
I bring my needs to you.

Remove all of my fear and anxiety that clouds my thoughts.
Expose the areas where the devil stirs up worry in my work.

Help me to see your constant provision for my business.

Show me what it means to seek first your kingdom
and righteousness with my business;
guide me in its application.

I want to be aligned with you and glorify you above all.

Let my business be a grand display of your faithfulness,
and help me to lead with confidence in you.

I trust you for all of our needs this week.

In the mighty name of Jesus, Amen.

———————●———————

Rely:_____

_____

_____

_____

_____

PRAYER

24

● Strength

Philippians 4:11–13

I have learned in whatever situation I am to be content. I know how to be brought low, and I know how to abound. In any and every circumstance, I have learned the secret of facing plenty and hunger, abundance and need. I can do all things through him who strengthens me.

Reflect: _____

_____

_____

_____

_____

Request: _____

_____

_____

_____

Rely: _____

_____

_____

_____

Heavenly Father,

Thank you for strengthening me when my strength fails.
I confess that I cannot accomplish your purpose
for my business in my strength.

Help me to be content when I am brought low.

I want to experience the confidence and security
that transcends my present circumstances.

Give me the strength to not be easily shaken.

Show me how to lead my business with
the same grace that you have shown me.

I want to trust you when business is low
and remember you when it abounds.

Make me steadfast in my faith, not swayed by lack or plenty.

I want my business to be empowered
by your strength and for your glory.

There is no obstacle too great and no challenge too big for you.

Reveal to me what you revealed to the Apostle Paul.

Show me how to do all things through your strength this week.

In the mighty name of Jesus, Amen.

■ **Direction**
■ **Strength**

Psalm 24:1–5

The earth is the Lord's and the fullness thereof,
the world and those who dwell therein. . . .
Who shall ascend the hill of the Lord?
And who shall stand in his holy place?
He who has clean hands and a pure heart,
who does not lift up his soul to what is false
and does not swear deceitfully.
He will receive blessing from the Lord
and righteousness from the God of his
salvation.

Reflect: _____
_____
_____
_____
_____
_____

Request: _____
_____
_____
_____
_____

Heavenly Father,

Thank you for inviting me into your plan
for the redemption of the world.

Just as everything in this world is ultimately yours,
I submit the ultimate ownership of my business to you.

I want to be an active participant in your purpose for my work.

Cause my business to prosper in your will and for your glory.

Give me clean hands and a pure heart and remove from me
everything that contradicts your character.

Unity with you is greater than any other form of success.

I commit myself to honesty, integrity, and diligence.
Show me how to do business in a way that reflects
your nature and the fruits of your spirit.

Pour out blessing and righteousness over my business
and all those that we influence.

Make my business a miracle that others would see
and glorify you this week.

In the mighty name of Jesus, Amen.

Rely:

PRAYER

26

■ **Wisdom**
■ **Direction**

2 Corinthians 5:16-18, 20

From now on, therefore, we regard no one according to the flesh. . . . If anyone is in Christ, he is a new creation. The old has passed away; behold, the new has come. All this is from God, who through Christ reconciled us to himself and gave us the ministry of reconciliation. . . . Therefore, we are ambassadors for Christ.

Reflect: _____

Request: _____

Rely: _____

Heavenly Father,

Thank you for making me a new creation.

I want my business to be one that operates
according to your values.

Help me not to recognize or judge others by worldly standards.
Show me how to see others as you see them.

Make my business part of your new creation
work with new ideas and innovation.

Fill us with faith in your promises
for ourselves and for those we work with.

Show me your higher purposes
for the relationships that you have given me at work.

Help me and my business be a true ambassador for Christ.
I want to represent you well to the watching world.

Make me a minister of reconciliation
and a vessel for your redemptive power.

Use me and my business to minister to the families of my
employees, vendors, customers, and community.

Help me to be an encourager to those around me this week.

In the mighty name of Jesus, Amen.

PRAYER

27

- **Strength**
- **Unity**

John 13:34-35

A new commandment I give to you, that you love one another: just as I have loved you, you also are to love one another. By this all people will know that you are my disciples, if you have love for one another.

Reflect: _____

_____

_____

_____

_____

Request: _____

_____

_____

_____

_____

_____

Heavenly Father,

Thank you for your unending love.

Expand my capacity to receive your love
so that I can truly love others as you love me.

Help me to better understand your love without any fear or doubt.

I trust your love and want to demonstrate it through my work.

Show me how to exhibit your love
in my business even in small ways.

May it be clear to everyone with whom
we interact that we do business differently.

Help us to value each person according to your love for them.

Show me how to run a business that would be
known by how we display your love.

Empower us to treat each other, every customer,
and our vendors with the same love as Jesus.

By love you overcame the world and claimed victory over death.
Help me to overcome the difficulties of this week
and find victory in your love.

In the mighty name of Jesus, Amen.

———————●———————

Rely:_____

_____

_____

_____

PRAYER

28

- **Strength**
- **Peace**

Colossians 3:12-1

Put on . . . compassionate hearts, kindness, humility, meekness, and patience, bearing with one another and . . . forgiving each other; as the Lord has forgiven you, so you also must forgive. And above all these put on love, which binds everything together in perfect harmony. And let the peace of Christ rule in your hearts, to which indeed you were called in one body. And be thankful. Let the word of Christ dwell in you richly, teaching and admonishing one another in all wisdom. . . . And whatever you do, in word or deed, do everything in the name of the Lord Jesus, giving thanks to God the Father through him.

Reflect: _____

_____

_____

_____

Request: _____

_____

_____

_____

Heavenly Father,

Thank you for your forgiveness.

I remember how you care for me better than I deserve.

Give me the grace to be compassionate,
kind, patient, and humble in my interactions at work.

I want my business to be consistent with your character.

Bring harmony to our workforce so that we may work as one.

Show me how to lead this business as if you led it.

Let your peace rule my heart.

Help me not to be easily shaken by my circumstances
but to have confidence in you.

I renounce the fear and doubt that gives me anxiety,
and I invite your peace into my heart and my business.

I lay my needs at your feet and ask for your wisdom and guidance.

Whatever I do this week, in word or deed,
I commit to doing with a thankful heart and for your glory.

In the mighty name of Jesus, Amen.

———————■———————

Rely: _____

_____

_____

_____

_____

29

▪ Provision

1 Corinthians 3:7-9

So neither he who plants nor he who waters is anything, but only God who gives the growth. He who plants and he who waters are one, and each will receive his wages according to his labor. For we are God's fellow workers. You are God's field, God's building.

Reflect: _____

_____

_____

_____

_____

_____

Request: _____

_____

_____

_____

_____

_____

Heavenly Father,

Thank you for giving me opportunities
for personal and professional growth
even when I don't recognize them.

Your plans produce the best growth.

I know that my business is healthiest in your hands.
Make me a vessel of the growth that comes from you.

Help me not to grow prideful or take credit for your provision.

Show me the areas of weakness where
I have relied on my strength at work.

Remove the distance between us and
make us fellow workers in your purpose.

Give us a fresh perspective of the work
that you are doing in us and through us.

I thank you for the small steps that have produced growth.

Stretch out your hand over the dormant areas of my
business and cause growth to spring forth.

May the barriers break and new growth to appear this week.

In the mighty name of Jesus, Amen.

———————————●———————————

Rely:_____

_____

_____

_____

PRAYER

30

- ## Strength
- ## Provision

2 Chronicles 16:8-9

[Have you not faced] a huge army with very many chariots and horsemen? Yet because you relied on the Lord, he gave them into your hand. For the eyes of the Lord run to and fro throughout the whole earth, to give strong support to those whose heart is blameless toward him.

Reflect: _____

_____

_____

_____

_____

_____

_____

Request: _____

_____

_____

_____

_____

_____

Heavenly Father,

Thank you for your goodness towards me.

I want to have a heart that is blameless towards you.

Help me with your grace and the power
of your Holy Spirit to live rightly before you.

In the midst of the challenges of my business,
I choose to rely on you.

I give my battles into your hands
and rely on you for a better outcome
than I could achieve on my own.

As your eyes search the earth,
I pray that my business and that I would
be a ready instrument in your hands.

Give us strong support as we seek to honor you in our work.

Let your favor rest on us so that others
would see our work and glorify you this week.

In the mighty name of Jesus, Amen.

———————●———————

Rely:_____

_____

_____

_____

_____

_____

PRAYER

31

- **Wisdom**
- **Direction**

Ecclesiastes 2:24-26

There is nothing better for a person than that he should . . . find enjoyment in his toil. This also, I saw, is from the hand of God, for apart from him who can . . . have enjoyment? For to the one who pleases him God has given wisdom and knowledge and joy, but to the sinner he has given the business of gathering and collecting, only to give to one who pleases God.

Reflect: _____

_____

_____

_____

_____

_____

Request: _____

_____

_____

_____

_____

_____

Heavenly Father,

Thank you for making work enjoyable when it is done with you.
It can be hard to find joy in my work apart from you.

Forgive me for the areas where I have
separated you from my business.

I want to find my greatest fulfillment in working together.

Help me to see simple steps to involve you in my workday.

Give me the wisdom to make the
best decisions to grow my business.

Give me the knowledge and connections
that I need to create new solutions to our challenges.

Give my employees and me the joy
that only comes from working with you.

I want to work and grow your way.

I ask for divine ideas and innovation,
divine appointments, and open doors.

May my business be blessed as I work with you this week.

In the mighty name of Jesus, Amen.

———————————●———————————

Rely:

PRAYER

32

■ Provision

Deuteronomy 30:9-10

The LORD your God will make you abundantly prosperous in all the work of your hand. . . . For the LORD will again take delight in prospering you, as he took delight in your fathers, when you obey the voice of the Lord your God, to keep his commandments and his statutes that are written in this Book of the Law, when you turn to the LORD your God with all your heart and with all your soul.

Reflect: _____

_____

_____

_____

_____

Request: _____

_____

_____

_____

_____

Heavenly Father,

Thank you for taking delight in providing for me.

It is easy to lose sight of your delight in the midst of the storms.

You are faithful even when I am faithless.

As a business leader, I want to honor you with my work
and achieve the kind of impact that only comes through you.

Show me how to lead my business according to your ways.

I commit to obey your voice and keep your commands
in the operation of my business.

I look to you for help and withhold nothing from you.

Have your way in my business and
make it abundantly prosperous for your glory.

Put your power on display to my
employees, vendors, and customers.

Help me to experience your delight in my work this week.

In the mighty name of Jesus, Amen.

———————■———————

Rely:_____

_____

_____

_____

_____

_____

PRAYER

33

James 4:1-3, 6

- **Provision**
- **Direction**

What causes quarrels and fights among you? Is it not this, that your passions are at war within you? You desire and do not have, so you murder. You covet and cannot obtain, so you fight and quarrel. You do not have because you do not ask. You ask and do not receive, because you ask wrongly, to spend it on your passions. . . . Therefore [Scripture] says, "God opposes the proud but gives grace to the humble."

Reflect: _____

_____

_____

_____

_____

Request: _____

_____

_____

_____

_____

Heavenly Father,

Thank you for always hearing my prayers.

You are always listening,
even when I don't feel like praying.

I want to invite you into the circumstances of my business.

I confess that I often strive to obtain in my own strength.
Help me to remember to take a moment to ask of you in prayer.

I don't want to miss out on answered prayer because I didn't ask.

Drive out the selfish pride that
pollutes my prayers and clouds my vision.

Make me passionate about what makes you passionate.

Give me a humble heart to glorify you with your provision.

I lift up the needs of my business this week
and ask you to provide as only you can do.

In the mighty name of Jesus, Amen.

———————

Rely:

PRAYER

34

● Peace

Philippians 4:5–7

The Lord is at hand [listening]; so do not be anxious about anything, but in everything by prayer and supplication with thanksgiving let your requests be made known to God. And the peace of God, which surpasses all understanding, will guard your hearts and your minds in Christ Jesus.

Reflect: _____

_____

_____

_____

_____

_____

_____

Request: _____

_____

_____

_____

_____

_____

Heavenly Father,

Thank you for your extravagant goodness.

You have made freedom from anxiety and stress
available to me through prayer.

I confess that there are moments and areas
of my business where anxiety controls me,
when I have not entrusted them to you in prayer.

I bring my burdens before you and ask for your help.

Stabilize me in these moments and help me
remember your promise to hear my prayers.

Help me to find you amid my storms rather
than avoiding them altogether.

I want your peace to guard my heart and mind as I trust in you.

Fill me with your Spirit and put my mind at rest.

Show me answers to prayer in my business this week.

In the mighty name of Jesus, Amen.

Rely:_____

_____

_____

_____

_____

35

- **Provision**
- **Strength**

2 Corinthians 12:9-10

He said to me, "My grace is sufficient for you, for my power is made perfect in weakness." Therefore I will boast all the more gladly of my weaknesses, so that the power of Christ may rest upon me. . . . For when I am weak, then I am strong.

Reflect: _____

_____

_____

_____

_____

_____

Request: _____

_____

_____

_____

_____

_____

Heavenly Father,

Thank you for sustaining me even when I don't deserve it.

I want to understand your grace in my business better.

They don't always feel sufficient in the moment,
but your grace, provision, and direction are always perfect.

Help me to embrace humility so that your strength
may be clearly seen in my work.

I surrender my business to you
and will boast of its dependence on you.

Let your power rest on me in my weakness.

If the outlook appears weak or uncertain,
I believe that the center of your will
is the strongest position for my business.

Cause us to prosper not because of my pride
but because of your grace.

Show yourself strong in my areas of weakness
and be glorified in my work this week.

In the mighty name of Jesus, Amen.

———————————

Rely:_____

_____

_____

_____

_____

36

- **Wisdom**
- **Strength**

Philippians 2:3-4

Do nothing from selfish ambition or conceit, but in humility count others more significant than yourselves. Let each of you look not only to his own interests, but also to the interests of others.

Reflect: _____

_____

_____

_____

_____

_____

_____

Request: _____

_____

_____

_____

_____

_____

_____

Heavenly Father,

Thank you for demonstrating true humility
through your sacrifice on the cross.

Help me to recognize when my selfish ambition
or conceit creeps into my work.

I look to the example of Jesus, who did not use others
for personal gain but invested in their success.

Protect my business from internal and
external forces of arrogance and pride.

Show me how to cultivate a business culture
with the humility of Jesus.

Give me the wisdom to find creative ways
to bless my employees, vendors, and customers.
Bless us as we care for others.

I want everyone we interact with to experience
a supernatural business culture empowered by you.

Help me operate my business in a way that demonstrates
your character and draws people to you this week.

In the mighty name of Jesus, Amen.

———————◾———————

Rely:_____

_____

_____

_____

_____

37

■ Provision

Malachi 3:10

*Bring the full tithe into the storehouse. . . .
And thereby put me to the test, says the
Lord of hosts, if I will not open the windows
of heaven for you and pour down for you a
blessing until there is no more need.*

Reflect: _____

_____

_____

_____

_____

Request: _____

_____

_____

_____

Rely: _____

_____

_____

_____

Heavenly Father,

Thank you for setting the example of generosity
through your generosity toward me.

I want to be faithful in giving
as you have been faithful in providing.

Show me when my fear or doubt gets in the way of your provision.

I commit today, as an act of faith,
to give as you have instructed me to give.

I want to be quick to give as you lead me,
holding your provision with an open hand.

Bless me and my business to be
a blessing to others through giving.

Make my business an example of how faithful giving
releases your blessing until there is no more need.

I want my business to receive your full blessing.

Use it as a miraculous testimony
of your provision through generosity.

I bring the needs of my business to you.

Open the windows of heaven
until there is no more need this week.

In the mighty name of Jesus, Amen.

PRAYER

38

- **Provision**
- **Strength**

Luke 6:35, 38

But love your enemies, and do good, and lend, expecting nothing in return, and your reward will be great. . . . Give, and it will be given to you. Good measure, pressed down, shaken together, running over, will be put into your lap. For with the measure you use it will be measured back to you.

Reflect: _____

_____

_____

_____

_____

_____

_____

Request: _____

_____

_____

_____

_____

_____

Heavenly Father,

Thank you for your goodness.

Though greed and competition pervade the world's
business culture, show me how to walk the higher road.

I want the conduct and operation of my business
to set an example of righteousness.

Help me to do good while my competitors conspire against me.

Help me to remain generous while others
seek to take advantage of me.

I want to do the right thing even if it puts me
at a disadvantage because I put my trust in you.

I withhold nothing from you.

Use my business to show the world
what it looks like to be underwritten by heaven.

Provide for us according to the riches of your glory this week.

In the mighty name of Jesus, Amen.

———————🔳———————

Rely:_____

_____

_____

_____

_____

PRAYER

39

● **Strength**

Proverbs 10:20-21

The tongue of the righteous is choice silver;
the heart of the wicked is of little worth.
The lips of the righteous feed many,
but fools starve for lack of sense.

Reflect: _____

_____

_____

_____

Request: _____

_____

_____

_____

Rely: _____

_____

_____

_____

Heavenly Father,

Thank you for your perfect leadership.

Help me to understand the power of my words.

Show me how the speech and language
of my business can contribute to our growth.

Give me opportunities to speak
words of life in every interaction.

Help me to control my tongue
and speak words of greater worth.

I want to lead our business culture
by the example of my words.

Empower us to overcome the habits
of complaining and bickering.

Instead, make our business culture
one of spoken encouragement and gratitude.

Show us how our communication
conveys value throughout our business.

Cause us to prosper through
the conduct of our speech this week.

In the mighty name of Jesus, Amen.

40

Proverbs 11:1, 6, 18

- **Provision**
- **Strength**

A false balance is an abomination to the Lord, but a just weight is his delight. . . . The righteousness of the upright delivers them, but the treacherous are taken captive by their lusts. . . . The wicked earns deceptive wages, but one who sows righteousness gets a sure reward.

Reflect: _____

_____

_____

_____

_____

_____

Request: _____

_____

_____

_____

_____

_____

Heavenly Father,

Thank you for your goodness and justice.

You delight in integrity and honesty in our work.

I admit it can be tempting to cut corners,
especially when the competition acts unfairly.

I want my business to stand out for your glory.

Make my business a light in the darkness
as we keep our ways straight.

I commit to lead my business with integrity.

Show me practical ways to align my business
with your righteousness.

Cleanse us of any area where
we have earned deceptive wages.

Help me to see righteous conduct as
an investment in a sure and eternal reward.

Bless us as we do things the right way,
even when those around us are dishonest.

Be glorified in the integrity of my business this week.

In the mighty name of Jesus, Amen.

————————●————————

Rely:_____

_____

_____

_____

PRAYER

41

- # Direction
- # Strength

Matthew 7:17-20

Every healthy tree bears good fruit, but the diseased tree bears bad fruit. A healthy tree cannot bear bad fruit, nor can a diseased tree bear good fruit. Every tree that does not bear good fruit is cut down and thrown into the fire. Thus you will recognize them by their fruits.

Reflect: _____

_____

_____

_____

_____

Request: _____

_____

_____

_____

_____

_____

Heavenly Father,

Thank you for giving my work greater meaning.

I want my business to be recognized by
its positive impact on everyone we interact with,
like a tree that is known by its fruit.

Make our products, services, and conduct a blessing
in the lives of our employees, vendors, and customers.

Show me how to improve the unhealthy areas of my business
that are not producing the best fruit.

Empower us to outperform the rest of our industry
in organizational health.

I want the quality of my work to be easily recognizable
and to represent you well.

Help me to build this business into a healthy tree
that is known for its quality in the community.

Go ahead of me as I work to represent you well this week.

In the mighty name of Jesus, Amen.

———————●———————

Rely: _____

_____

_____

_____

_____

PRAYER

42

- **Direction**
- **Peace**

Isaiah 48:16-18

Draw near to me, hear this:
from the beginning I have not spoken in
secret. . . . I am the Lord your God,
who teaches you to profit,
who leads you in the way you should go.
Oh that you had paid attention to my
commandments!
Then your peace would have been like a river,
and your righteousness like the waves of the
sea.

Reflect: _____

_____

_____

_____

_____

Request: _____

_____

_____

_____

_____

Heavenly Father,

Thank you for delighting in me.

Help me to draw near to you in confidence
and to ignore the accusation of the devil.

Speak to me and let me hear your voice more clearly.

Lead me in the way that I should go with my work.

I invite you to guide my business,
and I commit to obey your commands.

Show me how to lead like you.

Teach me how to be profitable in your eternal economy
and how to make my business a blessing to others.

Give me peace like a river for my restlessness,
and show me the ripple effect of my business
in the lives that we serve.

I put my trust in you as my provider and teacher.

Let me hear your voice this week.

In the mighty name of Jesus, Amen.

Rely:_____

_____

_____

_____

_____

43

Matthew 6:19-21, 24

■ Wisdom

Do not lay up for yourselves treasures on earth, where moth and rust destroy and where thieves break in and steal, but lay up for yourselves treasures in heaven, where neither moth nor rust destroys and where thieves do not break in and steal. For where your treasure is, there your heart will be also. . . . You cannot serve both God and money.

Reflect: _____

_____

_____

_____

_____

_____

Request: _____

_____

_____

_____

_____

_____

_____

Heavenly Father,

Thank you for giving me eternal treasures.

Search me, and show me the areas of my life
where I am living for earthly treasures.

I want to lead my business with a heart that is loyal to you.

Teach me how to lay up treasures in heaven
and how to invest in eternal rewards.

Give me faith to prioritize heaven's ROI over earthly gain.

Guide me with your wisdom to use the resources
that you have entrusted me to for eternal significance.

You are my greatest treasure, and I commit my earthly resources
to the purpose for which you have provided them.

Use my business to make heavenly investments
in the lives of others this week.

In the mighty name of Jesus, Amen.

Rely:

PRAYER

44

- **Provision**
- **Direction**

2 Corinthians 9:6-8

The point is this: whoever sows sparingly will also reap sparingly, and whoever sows bountifully will also reap bountifully. Each one must give as he has decided in his heart, not reluctantly or under compulsion, for God loves a cheerful giver. And God is able to make all grace abound to you, so that having all sufficiency in all things at all times, you may abound in every good work.

Reflect: _____

_____

_____

_____

_____

_____

Request: _____

_____

_____

_____

_____

_____

Heavenly Father,

Thank you for your abounding grace in my business,
even when I don't recognize it.

Lead me in how I should give of the resources
that you have entrusted to me.

Show me where to sow bountifully to bear the greatest fruit.

Excite my heart about where to give
and help me to be a cheerful giver.

Make my business characterized by contagious generosity
that attracts the provision of heaven.

Help me to trust you to provide as I give where you lead.

I want to be about your business.

Make us sufficient in all things so that we can abound
in every good work this week.

In the mighty name of Jesus, Amen.

———————🔳———————

Rely:_____

_____

_____

_____

_____

_____

PRAYER
45

Psalm 127:1-2

● **Direction**
● **Strength**

Unless the Lord builds the house,
those who build it labor in vain.
Unless the Lord watches over the city,
the watchman stays awake in vain.
It is in vain that you rise up early
and go late to rest,
eating the bread of anxious toil;
for he gives to his beloved sleep.

Reflect: _____

_____

_____

_____

_____

_____

Request: _____

_____

_____

_____

_____

Heavenly Father,

Thank you for watching over me.

I have felt the anxiety and strain of
building my business in my strength.

I want to experience the joy of work with you.

I invite you into the process of building my business.

Show me your plans and purposes for my work.

Teach me how to lead and grow my business in healthy ways.

Shape it into something that only you could build,
and that would inspire others.

Guard me against the temptation
to rely on myself for success apart from you.

You are our chief builder and provider.

Help me to rest in your provision this week.

In the mighty name of Jesus, Amen.

Rely:_____

_____

_____

_____

_____

_____

PRAYER

46

- **Direction**
- **Peace**

Psalm 112:1, 3-4

Blessed is the man who fears the Lord,
who greatly delights in his
commandments! . . .
Wealth and riches are in his house,
and his righteousness endures forever.
Light dawns in the darkness for the upright;
he is gracious, merciful, and righteous.

Reflect: _____

_____

_____

_____

_____

_____

_____

_____

Request: _____

_____

_____

_____

_____

_____

Heavenly Father,

Thank you for your grace and mercy.

Help me to honor you with my work
and delight in your commandments.

Show me how to lead my business
according to your will and your ways.

Don't let my foot stumble from your path,
because your path is where I want to be.

I want to have the righteousness
that outlasts every other form of success.

Help me and my business to be characterized
as gracious, merciful, and righteous.

In my darkest moments, when I face my greatest challenges,
as anxiety besets me, fill me with your Spirit like the light of dawn.

I want my faith to be stable in every circumstance.

Provide for my business according
to the riches of your glory this week.

In the mighty name of Jesus, Amen.

———————●———————

Rely: _____

_____

_____

_____

_____

PRAYER

47

● **Strength**
● **Peace**

Psalm 112:5-8

It is well with the man who deals generously
and lends;
who conducts his affairs with justice.
For the righteous will never be moved;
he will be remembered forever.
He is not afraid of bad news;
his heart Is firm, trusting in the Lord
His heart is steady; he will not be afraid,
until he looks in triumph on his adversaries.

Reflect: _____

_____

_____

_____

_____

Request: _____

_____

_____

_____

Rely: _____

_____

_____

Heavenly Father,

Thank you for dealing generously with me.

I want my life and my business to reflect your goodness.

Enable me to recognize your generosity
and demonstrate it to others in greater ways.

I commit again to conduct my business
with integrity in the unseen areas.

Show me how to lead a righteous business
that cannot be moved, and that will be remembered forever.

I rely on you for stability and security.

Give me the kind of faith that drives out fear.

I want my heart to be firm, as I trust in you.

Reveal to me the areas of my business
where I have not trusted fully in you.

Help me not to be fearful when challenges arise
and give me the grace to react with faith.

Make your power so evident that even
our adversaries will marvel and glorify you.

May your will be done, and your kingdom come
in my work this week.

In the mighty name of Jesus, Amen.

PRAYER

48

■ **Wisdom**
■ **Hope**

Psalm 39:4-7

O Lord, make me know my end
and what is the measure of my days. . . .
Behold, you have made my days a few
handbreadths,
and my lifetime is as nothing before you. . . .
Man heaps up wealth and does not know
who will gather!
And now, O Lord, for what do I wait?
My hope is in you.

Reflect: _____

_____

_____

_____

_____

_____

_____

Request: _____

_____

_____

_____

_____

Heavenly Father,

Thank you for giving meaning to my days, limited as they are.

I am reminded today that every day is in your hands,
and only you know their measure.

Only you have the perfect micro-level and
macro-level perspective of my business.

Give me your vision.
Show me how to work with eternal significance
in alignment with your vision for my business.

I want my work to be about more than endless accumulation.

My hope does not come from a
balance sheet or external circumstances.

My hope is in you! Nothing else will satisfy like seeing
your purpose accomplished through my work.

Make my work a legacy through the lives that we improve
among our employees, vendors, customers, and community.

Provide for our needs and give us your perspective
for all that we do this week.

In the mighty name of Jesus, Amen.

Rely:_____

_____

_____

_____

_____

49

- **Provision**
- **Direction**

Psalm 145:15-19

The eyes of all look to you,

and you give them their food in due season.

You open your hand; you satisfy the desire

of every living thing. The Lord is righteous in

all his ways and kind in all his works.

The Lord is near to all who call on him,

to all who call on him in truth.

He fulfills the desire of those who fear him;

he also hears their cry and saves them.

Reflect: _____

_____

_____

_____

_____

_____

Request: _____

_____

_____

_____

Heavenly Father,

Thank you, Lord, that I can look to you
for direction and provision.

Be near to my business this week as we work your way.

I trust you for every need in my business.

Make this the due season of harvest and
provide for us from your hand.

Your lovingkindness is better than any worldly success.

I cannot be satisfied apart from you.

Correct me in any area that hinders your will for my work.

Give us an advantage in our areas of struggle
and be strong where we are weak.

Guide me through each meeting and decision
so that you might be glorified through our work.

Align me with your desire and empower me
to accomplish it this week.

In the mighty name of Jesus, Amen.

———————●———————

Rely:_____

_____

_____

_____

_____

50

- **Protection**
- **Strength**

Psalm 84:5-7, 11

Blessed are those whose strength is in you,
in whose heart are the highways to Zion
[heaven].
As they go through the valley of Baca
[weeping]
they make it a place of springs. . . . They go
from strength to strength;
each one appears before God in Zion. . . .
For the Lord God is a sun and shield;
the Lord bestows favor and honor.
No good thing does he withhold
from those who walk uprightly.

Reflect: _____

_____

_____

_____

_____

Request: _____

_____

_____

_____

_____

Heavenly Father,

Thank you for giving me a highway to heaven through prayer.

I confess that my strength is not in myself
or my bank account, but in you.

Give me your strength and your blessing in my work.

I trust you as my sun and shield, the provider,
and protector of my business.

Give me faith in moments of uncertainty
when things do not go according to plan.

Turn our challenging circumstances
into blessings that draw us closer to you.

Cause my business to grow from strength to strength
because of your faithfulness.

Withhold no good thing from me
as I commit myself to do business your way.

Release your provision and give me favor
and honor at work this week.

In the mighty name of Jesus, Amen.

———————●———————

Rely:_____

_____

_____

_____

_____

Take Inventory Six Months Later . . .

At the beginning of your journey, you completed a short series of inventory questions regarding your business. Now after six months, take a moment to update your responses using the space below. You can revisit your initial responses on pages 16-19 to compare your answers.

Since you began, what has changed?

_____

_____

_____

_____

_____

_____

_____

Have you recognized more answered prayer since you began? sIf so, list some examples.

_____

_____

_____

_____

_____

_____

_____

_____

What do you now imagine that God thinks about your business? How is your answer different than your initial answer?

_____

_____

_____

_____

_____

_____

_____

_____

_____

_____

What would you now say is God's purpose for your business?

_____

_____

_____

_____

_____

_____

_____

_____

_____

_____

What insight have you received regarding your one particular thing? (You can continue to ask for insight on that same topic, or list a new topic below.)

_____

_____

_____

_____

_____

_____

_____

_____

_____

Having sought the Lord for these six months, take a look back at your previous list of obstacles and opportunities. Note your progress.

_____

_____

_____

_____

_____

_____

_____

_____

_____

_____

Now look ahead to the next six months.

Update your obstacles and opportunities. It is okay if the list is the same now as when you started. Don't give up! Don't forget to celebrate what God has done! What might the Lord be saying to you about the next six months or year? What would his goals to pursue for your business?

About the Author

Logan Bloom is a connector and intercessor who is dedicated to serving leaders. His passion is to connect leaders to realize the potential of their collective impact. Since 2007, Logan has been equipping leaders in every social sector in the spirit of Jesus. Logan has a nonprofit background and he now serves as part of CityChurch Network. He lives in Little Rock, Arkansas, with his wife and two children.

CityChurch Network

Building on the foundation of a twenty-year movement of prayer and serving our city, CityChurch Network is a multi-denominational, multi-ethic gospel movement uniting churches through extraordinary prayer, trained leaders, and collective impact.

citychurchar.org

Sign up to receive weekly prayers for your business via email at **servantleadernetwork.org**.

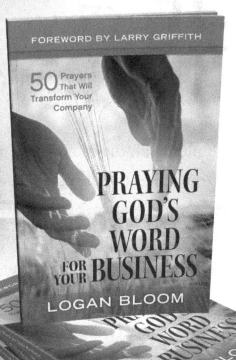

Put

Praying God's Word for Your Business

into the hands of business owners and executives you know.

Equip them to seek God's blessing, wisdom and direction over their business, too.

Multiple-copy discounts are available at prayershop.org

PRAYERSHOP PUBLISHING

Pray for Your City

Many intercessors and leaders in communities across the country are learning how to pray effectively for their cities. If a city prospers, its businesses will prosper, too. *City of Prayer: Transform Your Community Through Praying Churches,* will inspire and equip you to be a catalyst for prayer in your city.

Multiple-copy discounts available at prayershop.org

*Prayer*CONNECT

A QUARTERLY MAGAZINE DESIGNED TO:

Mobilize believers to pray God's purposes for their church, city and nation.

Connect intercessors with the growing worldwide prayer movement.

Equip prayer leaders and pastors with tools to disciple their congregations.

Each issue of *Prayer Connect* includes:

- Practical articles to equip and inspire your prayer life.
- Helpful prayer tips and proven ideas.
- News of prayer movements around the world.
- Theme articles exploring important prayer topics.
- Connections to prayer resources available online.

Print subscription: $24.99 (includes digital version)

Digital subscription: $19.99

Church Prayer Leaders Network membership: $35.99 (includes print, digital, and CPLN membership benefits)

SUBSCRIBE NOW.
www.prayerleader.com/membership or call 800-217-5200